STRANGER, BABY

EMILY BERRY

Stranger, Baby

FABER & FABER

First published in the UK in 2017
First published in the USA in 2017
by Faber & Faber Ltd
Bloomsbury House
74–77 Great Russell Street
London WC1B 3DA

Typeset by Hamish Ironside
Printed in England by TJ Books Limited, Padstow, Cornwall

A CIP record for this book is available from the British Library

ISBN 978–0–571–33132–1

Contents

The loss of a mother must be something very strange . . .
Sigmund Freud, tr. Tania and James Stern

STRANGER, BABY

Sign of the Anchor

I stood at the dangerous shore.
Sleeves rolled up to my shoulders.
My fringe lifted in the wind in a long salute and I pushed it back.
Live your wish, Live your wish, said the sea.
I wanted to be like the shells on the beach, rubbed smooth and
    cracked open.
And I held my arms out, tipped my head back, pictured my
    protective symbols.
I opened my eyes and saw the sign of the anchor burning.
I had to go.
I shouted some words but they were lost when the waves crashed.
And ash rained from the sky.
I was far out, in wet denim, and the shore was a jolt when I
    looked back.

Picnic

If you are not happy, the sea is not happy
It sulks in and out of the bay
I lie on the bed or stand at the window watching the sea
Why must we destroy what we do
Watching the sea is like watching something in pieces
    continually striving to be whole
Imagine trying to pick up a piece of the sea and show it to a person
I tried to do that
All that year I visited a man in a room
I polished my feelings
Sometimes I think if the devil came and offered to swap me into
    some other body without me knowing what I'd be getting, I'd
    say . . . *Sure*
And, sure, I believe in the devil

I wanted to love the world
I thought when all the anxiety slipped away, I'd watch it go, and I'd
    know precisely
Every increment of its departure
The way 'getting better' can be an unfolding
The covers pulled back, the light coming in

        *

    The mood of the sea is catching
Your eyes wear out from all the glitches
I sat there watching it and I can assure you it is so
Its colour became the colour of my eyes and the salt made me cry
    oceans

        *

I like curved things
    Apples, peaches, the crest of a wave
We once agreed the apple was the only iconic fruit

I like it when I am writing a poem and I know that I am feeling
    something
To be poised and to invite contact
Or to appear to invite contact

    Remember when we used to imagine
    Our correspondence would make us famous or that
    Once we'd become famous our correspondence would too?
    Maybe it still will
    I'll need to make a lot of cuts first

When did everybody start wanting to be famous all the time
Or has it always been this way
This is the rain, the October rain
I wrote that when it was still October
It must have been raining

This is sadness: men in waterproofs dragging the deep lake
The warm American voice says: *There is no lack or limitation,*
    there is only error in thought
My thoughts are wrong. My thoughts are wrong
The thought that my thoughts are wrong is wrong

       *

I started to be able to see in the dark
It hurt my eyes
        My, yes, salty, wet, ocean-coloured eyes
Albeit that in the dark they were the colour of the dark, and on fire

       *

When the rain came after the drought they said it was not good
   enough
It would not change things
It was the wrong rain
The rain came out of my eyes and fell on the ground and dried up

Who are you. Who are you. Who are you

Stop, language is crawling all over me
Sometimes if you stay still long enough you can make it go
If a person standing still watched another person minutely moving
   would it seem after a while as if they were watching the sea?
I remember just one thing my mother said to me:
Never look at yourself in the mirror when you're crying
    I did not follow her advice

Summer

In a kitchen, on an island, stirring tomato sauce, I am far from home.

I stir the thickening tomato sauce.

Deadly kitchen, which is hot with the temperament of this country, and with the heat of cooking.

Deadly sauce, which thickens with my sinking feeling. Which cracks my ice caps.

And now they let out a scream.

I am thirteen years away from home. Later, twenty, and so on.

I can't get back.

Someone is holding me and crying. Greek sunset.

From now on I will eat only the foods of the region that require no preparation, that cannot break into me: white cheese, white bread.

Colour all over my hands, I get down on the floor of a tiled, white room.

'She had it'

(a cut-out)

She had it
all cut off
It was more suitable
If only I
could see
my mother
when it is dark,
I can see
only myself
She won't come,
they can remove
even this
cut it off.

Tragedy for One Voice

ACT ONE

[*Alone onstage with a coffin. Windchimes*]

ME ONE: There is a part of me that will always miss what I lost

ME TWO: They all said the same thing in their letters. *Poor little ____. I hope she will be okay, poor little ____*

ME ONE: I went back to the burned house

ME TWO: Day of the week: immaterial. Time of year: immaterial

ME ONE: Who was there: me and another girl, also me (you) [*gesturing to* ME TWO]

ME TWO: [*angry*] During leave-taking from mother: 'without ceremony, the children were far more distressed than if mother left with the proper rituals'

CHORUS: Give us this day our proper rituals! Give us some fucking ceremony!

[*Curtain*]

ACT TWO

[*A kind of light that is not the right kind of light; screaming*]

ME ONE: Somebody said: 'I am a master of elision.' I veiled my tended wound. I veiled my narrative. Somebody called it: 'some kind of gratuitous beauty'. I veiled my photograph of her in sixties playsuit

ME TWO: Somebody wrote: 'Thereafter, hidden away, in some locked cupboard of the mind, he carries the murderous dead thing within him, an unappeased *Doppelgänger*, not to be placated, crying out to be heard'

ME ONE: I GIVE BIRTH TO MURDEROUS DEAD THING let it go to swimming pools, meditation sessions, take it on train journeys during which I feel ABANDONED and ALONE—

CHORUS: I was so small! I was so capable!

ME ONE: I run out into the street. I find someone. I tell them everything. 'I have got it in me!' I shout. 'Undigested! Whole! The dead body of a woman! I am conducting a murder investigation! Victim performed disappearing act leaving empty shell and devastation!'

ME TWO: Why didn't I—

ME ONE: I'm sorry

ME TWO: What for

ME ONE: For myself

[*Sound of breaking strings*]

ME TWO + CHORUS (*of baritones*): —*SAVE HER*

[*Curtains*]

The End

I believed death was a flat plain spectacular endlessly

Can you distort my voice when I say this?

My scared ghost peeling off me

Distortion, she says, as if she has just made it up

And then she is quoting a line from a poem

Or is it a whole poem, I wish I could remember

My voice opens and calls you in

I don't know if you can hear me

I said, I carry inside me the trace of a threat that I cannot
discharge

I said, I want to ask you things you can't ask a person who
doesn't exist

She said, Why can't you ask them

If we can't have everything what is the closest amount to
everything we can have?

She said, Why can't you have everything

Well, you know, when you're looking for a person, sometimes
    they appear

And a light goes on and off in the opposite window, twice

Yes, you say, that was a sign

Strange love for the living, strange love for the dead

Listen. I don't know who you are but you remind me of—

I wish you would put some kind of distortion on my voice,
    I tell her

So people don't know it's me

They know what they know, she said

I told a story about my shame

It got cold when the air touched it

Then it got hot, throbbed, wept, attracted fragments with
    which it eventually glittered

Till I couldn't stop looking at it

Exactly, she says

And then she is quoting a line from a poem, I don't know
which one

In my dream she reached out to touch me as if to say, It's all
right

How I began to believe in something

Are you there?

The wind called to the trees

And then it happened

And they said, How do you feel?

And I said, Like a fountain

Night falls from my neck like silver arrows

Very gently

Winter

When the new room was built my mother showed me What To Do In Case Of Fire. There were four metal rungs embedded in the balcony wall: this was the escape route. She did not show me (then) the other one.

What happened was, my mother was very very sad. She was so sad she could not hold up her head, she could not sit down, she could not lie down, she could not see out of the dark, my very sad mum.

In the course of my research I learned a new kind of love. This lesson taught me to pray. I made a prayer for my mother. By 'prayer' I mean a meditation on a want that can never be answered. A prayer for the dead alive inside the living. That's what it is to burn a flame. We were in the darkest days of winter, approaching the celebration of light.

I watched the white men in their pastel coats / Roll you up and put you away / They put you inside their white box / With its clicks and locks / And carried you far away

Part

I wanted to put my body into these words
I wanted this to be a part of my body
This part of my body

Everything Bad Is Permanent

Their eyes are grey. My eyes are grey
My wishes are the colour of the dead in numbers

My dying, undelivered wishes. Ours
Would somebody come running. Would they

Prototypes of human sorrow
Protest, despair and detachment

Blank, tearful retreat from mother
Mother, Baby. Stranger, Baby. Baby Alone

I was completing a form that said rate my *unhealthy emotions*
It was some kind of duty, or project

Some people don't put question marks at the ends of questions
   any more
In case anyone should think they'd be so idealistic as to expect
   an answer

Then, looking reproachfully at her mother, she demanded
'Where was you, Mummy? Where was *you?'*

Where was you, Mummy
As when from a stable place you come unbalanced

I did it once by accident, now I do it deliberately, in plain sight
In decorated sight

Is hate a viable form of activism
The place where hate of the self meets hate of the other (for
    example), who claims that land

I wrote: The sea! The sea! as if that might be a solution
Didn't we always suspect the pain of intelligent people was
    truly the most painful

Forgive me quickly/forget me quickly
I know that I must forget *you*

The sea is somewhere anything can happen
You know when two seas come together there is deep pain and
    pleasure at the border

Tremor of conjoined hopes. Agony of separation after mixing.
    Let it flow
I sat down. Wrote: GUILT 90% SHAME 90% RAGE 90%
    FEAR 90% LOVE—

(I never once dreamed of you
Why did I never

And now I have a question for you, will you answer?
And there you were all this time, in the dead ground)

Song

after Luna Miguel

When I became mermaid it was for this reason.
The girl I love is a beautiful boy.
So you would not ask questions.
Because I gave myself up to the rain
but it was too late; the rain could not save me.
And when I thought the line was straight,
I was wrong; I could not follow the line.
Thus the shore, infinitely. Thus these rocks.
There was so much to feel good and sorry about.
And I shut my legs up tight, I shut my eyes.
So I could see him better, so I could see her.

Aqua

I filled a bowl
with a little
water praised
it slightly a feeling
of daughterliness
came over me
I adored her
of course water
cannot hold
an imprint she
kept repeating
*it's no use you
can't help me*
something close
to the surface a
terrible sense of
violence when
waves travel into
shallow water
they begin to be
affected by the
ocean bottom
the wave breaks
is translated into
another wave
*singular and
beautiful phenomenon*
erosion of the
ocean bottom
intensifies I am

able to hear these
painful reminiscences
with a little more
detachment I said
unconvincingly
it should be easy
to float away I
wish to be immersed
and live forever
on the cusp of
drowning it's no
way to abide I knelt
down drank this
exalted element
her ghost took
many forms
sometimes she
came down as
rain that was
the most benign
other times she came
close to killing me
what a beautiful
sentence I must
write that down in
my book I adored
her of course it was
a lovely sunny day

Tidal Wave Speaks

This is what I did.
Laid it all out like tidal wave.
Thought you could in fact
lay out a tidal wave.

Coming for me. Coming for you.
Thought, with the right attitude, you could train it to sing.
My hands were wet.
My face was wet.

Tidal Wave don't sing, said Tidal Wave.
Tidal Wave crash.

Now all my poems are about death I feel
as though I'm really living

Under the trees, on the wet ground, with the staggering crows.

I photograph myself in the cemetery.

I kneel and speak to you and I observe myself doing it.

The crows observe themselves.

The dead can answer us only in our own words.

Can you imagine? Of course, you can't imagine.

Your silence reaches out from inside me and meets itself on the outside.

A sign says: Some memorials may be unstable.

But what is the silence *like*, someone wanted to know.

Tell us something, in your own inimitable style.

It's raining in the cemetery.

I pose and yet I cannot pose.

I knelt, I spoke, I cried, I wrote this down, regretted it.

New Project

All day every day
with this in mind
dialled up to
unbearable
frequency I
rang nonstop
thoughts so
hard they must
have shown
sometimes they
stuck out mostly
they stuck in
I had never
we all say that
don't we
I had never
felt this way
I was led totally
strung out every
nerve onboard
yet I could
not be sure
what actually
this was, like
my mother wearing
someone else's
ghost a surface
with the sun
shining off it
a mirror maybe

just a fucking
mirror or was I
just at the start
of a new project

T

This hope   with Australian wild peach
          is what keeps me going
               I spell your name
with macadamia nut   never mind jojoba
                              One oil is the aroma
the other is the carrier   Often I wonder:
          how does the carrier feel?
          I always see hierarchy
Some letters of the alphabet, for example
are more powerful   T is one
T is such a strong character . . .

          Top note, heart note, base note:
which would you rather be?   I call my dad
to ask what botanicals were in vogue in his day
Whenever I pick up the phone I hear the sea
          Maybe balsam? he says
Sometimes the last one you think of
          is the one who'll know

So

that
was
your
attempt
at
dying
which
I
am
still
embarrassed
by
is
it
not
so
terribly
gauche
to
die

The photo that is most troubling is the one
I don't want to show you

Breathing, distraction, whatever
I lay down in this field
I stopped agonising because it started to seem as if agonising
    was hurting me
'The dead don't die. They look on and help.'
Excuse these intense but beautiful bouts of emotion
I seem to be gradually coming to some realisations
And I didn't know what to make of it at the time
My mouth opened and I breathed flame
Mother, can you hear me?
He said, *The dead don't die!*
It was dark and something was kind of starry
Ardent . . .
Something as auspicious as a child born on my birthday
It wasn't in the normal run of things
But I hold her
I hold her the way I reach inside myself and hold all the trouble
Skies suddenly so dark
And the way home on fire
Through the forest, loud and forgetful as a burst of rain
In case you could hear me
On the backs of horses

Once

When I refused
once it became
ever easier to
keep on refusing
it came to seem
as though refusal
was in fact a way
of embracing I
became so quiet
what exactly I
embraced is hard
to say I suppose
it was my own
diminishment
which seemed
rare & requiring
tenderness so I
sent my loved ones
away & kindly they
went I imagined
them active in my
absence & it was
like rehearsing my
death their capacity
for survival was thus
proved & mine too
insultingly so

Two Rooms

I went into one room and then I went into another.
I was in a room inside a room.
There I felt safe.

Freud's War

I became a therapist against my will
A strange feeling of forlornness, a feeling I could not have
    stood
Painful isolation, quite steep and slanting
A beautiful forest which had the one drawback of seeming
    never to end
I have had to struggle so long
I have always been frank with you, haven't I?
I wanted to explain the reason for my inaccessibility
I am lying here on a short leash in this filthy hole
So far I haven't been locked up
Several people point to gaps in my face where the little girl has
    been cut out
She screams and screams without any self-control
Ravaged by the heat and the blood-&-thunder melodrama
Neither describable nor bearable
I felt I had known her all my life

Freud's Beautiful Things

I have some sad news for you
I am just a symbol, a shadow cast on paper
If only you knew how things look within me at the moment
Trees covered in white blossom
The remains of my physical self
Do you really find my appearance so attractive?
Darling, I have been telling an awful lot of lies lately
If only I knew what you are doing now?
Standing in the garden and gazing out into the deserted street?
Not a mermaid, but a lovely human being
The whole thing reminds me of the man trying to rescue a
    birdcage from the burning house
(I feel compelled to express myself poetically)
I am not normally a hunter of relics, but . . .
It was this childhood scene . . .
(My mother . . .)
All the while I kept thinking: *her face has such a wild look*
. . . as though she had never existed
The fact is I have not yet seen her in daylight
Distance must remain distance
A few proud buildings; your lovely photograph
I find this loss very hard to bear
The bells are ringing, I don't quite know why
What makes all autobiographies worthless is, after all, their
    mendacity
Yesterday and today have been bad days
This oceanic feeling, continuous inner monologues
I said, 'All the beautiful things I still have to say will have to
    remain unsaid', and the writing table flooded

Freud's Horses

Until nightfall I was with the dead
We either had to go all the way back or stay down below
For none of us can life be made any safer
Horses break loose, hailstones of a fantastic size beat against
    the windows
And we hadn't the courage
Everything comes to an end
Today's rain
I am thinking of eating a pomegranate

Freud's Loss

You climb a hill as high as the Leopoldsburg
The road is so narrow that only a light little carriage can go up it
The carriage can't hold more than two people: a mother and a child
There is a kind of holy Sunday stillness over everything
Huge mountains, some overgrown, some bare in strange formation
You must imagine it like this:
A two and a half hour journey through the most desolate lagoons
A magnificent river
Vaults, waterfalls, stalactites
Sorry that I have to write about such sad things!
To mourn . . . is of course permissible
On our way back it began to rain, but gently
The rest – you will know what I mean – is silence

Girl on a Liner

after Rose Wylie

This is the body's way of handling emotion.
I am dreaming a lot about voyages.
Mostly I can't remember them. There is something spilled
in the background (they say it is a house).
I wrote, *Nothing in the outside world is changed*,
to ward off the catastrophe. I am in a beautiful place
with birdsong and which smells of flowers; yet,
everything very skewed. I loved you, but not in a pure way.
Something kitsch could break my heart so thoroughly.
Why should it not? '"What do you want?" is not a simple question!'
I say, again, or am I shouting. But you must know,
they said, calmly and like a very light breeze.
You must have some idea. What's that noise?
I expect it's the sound of the train breaking down.
Does crying age one? If so I suppose I've become very old.
In the dream there is something hard he is asking me
(my father) but it's vague . . . it's vague. I examine my face
in the morning. It is only partly like hers.
I watch the water pour out of my eyes; there was a feeling
but I wrote it down and it ceased to be a feeling,
became art. '"I am afraid of . . ."' they explained,
'might be better rendered as, "There is a fear of . . ."' Then
I get confused-stroke-scared, looking at the shit-coloured night,
and there's a curt wind at my back and I'm crying again,
crying with the relief of not being loved. *Whatever it is*
will reveal itself, but I feel like that grubby place
beneath the door handle, the place everyone touches

as they leave. Sometimes the world goes very hard
and cannot be got into; I slide off its surfaces
and I am trying to take in air, or trying not to.
I cannot believe I would conceive of doing that to you.
In the house she is very plaintive and timid, bereft,
and goes into a room off a long corridor,
making mournful noises. I feel terrible. I'm standing
on the edge of nothing, with a handkerchief,
in a ball gown, and I am waving goodbye to you all.

Sleeping

after Paula Rego

That's what we do in the desert.

I love it most when I'm asleep.

I don't like it under the sun, with a desert bird to escape from.

I don't like it unless my sisters love me.

And they do, but I forget.

When they don't wake up I forget.

Then there's only my mother on her knees with her apron lifted to catch the world if it goes wrong.

It went wrong and she didn't catch it.

The desert bird opened its beak and I got dizzy. This way I feel.

I leant over all heavy and one side of my hair hung down.

This is why we fall asleep in the desert, because we are full of pain.

I shout at her, Mother, why you always turned away?

She says, Because of the ocean.

All the times I didn't know if this was my life.

If it was up to me, I would not have her back.

It is not up to me, and she is not coming back.

Both my sisters sleeping as if at peace, and still I forget how much they love me, because they cannot stay awake for me.

See how hard and red the ground is.

And we're so scared.

My mother's final arrangement with hope.

I pray to the desert bird, There must be another way to die, one that hurts less.

Drunken Bellarmine

after Renee So

In this spirit of affliction I beheld two things,
that shame is also revelry, and a body
is a spillage, or an addiction. I do not know
if this thing belongs to me, tipped-up set of weights
that promises, but never delivers, equilibrium.
I cannot make manifest this collection of feelings,
but look at me: I want to be loved for the wrong reasons.
I mean I want to be hated for the right reasons.
I have been lonely. Every time I say the word 'I'
I am ashamed. When I say 'I want' I am triply
ashamed. I want my shame to be a kind of proof
that deduces the world, and that's the worst
shame of all. I have been theatrical, entropic,
parting with myself for company. This heartsore
will not stop weeping and look, the sky is sick,
knitted too tightly; my face is up your sleeve
like a card trick. *DON'T LOVE ME*: I am guilty,
fatalistic and sticky round the mouth like a dirty baby.
I am a shitting, leaking, bloody clump of cells,
raw, murky and fluorescent, you couldn't take it.

Flowers

When I was
being haunted
it was as though
you had come
back from the
dead but would
not visit me
I learnt that
haunting was
what happened
when I let my
want escape
violent beams
of coloured light
at first it seemed
like a miracle
the first stain
that bloodstain
the little bell
the quiet night
no shortage of
flowers I let a
long pause elapse
then we dragged
the body outside

The Whole Show

I PREFER TO DELAY MOVING ON TO THE NEXT STAGE
I SEE MYSELF WATCHING FOR MYSELF
WATCHING MYSELF COMING FOR MY SELF
IF ONLY I COULD SEE SOME END IN SIGHT
I THINK THEN I
MIGHT BE ABLE TO ENDURE IT
I FEAR THAT MY ALLY IS REALLY MY ENEMY
AND THE WAY THE CAT'S EYES ALWAYS
KEEP SHUTTING
HE MUST FIND MY PRESENCE VERY PAINFUL
I WOULD NOT LIKE TO THINK THAT I HAD BEEN
   TAKEN
WHEN I WAS NOT READY TO GO
YOU COULD ASK FOR FORGIVENESS
A GOOD DEED
AND ONE DAY I SHALL BRING
BEFORE IT WAS TOO LATE
MYSELF TO GO

*

I AM SOMETIMES AFRAID
SOMETIMES
ALL THE LONG DAY
AT NIGHT
COLD WITH MY BARE FEET
AND THEN IT IS SO TERRIFYING
BUT SCREW MY COURAGE
I KNOW THEY WILL COME TOMORROW
THEY WILL

*

I HAVE AN UNKNOWN ALLY
I WISH I KNEW WHO YOU WERE
I LACK THE COURAGE TO KNOW
YOUR HAIR SOFTLY NIGHT-TIME
IN A PALE BLUE SILK GOWN

*

WHEN THE TIME COMES
I MIGHT BE ABLE TO ENDURE IT
I KNOW MYSELF I PREFER
MYSELF
THE WAY THE STEAM RISES
AND THE WAY THE CAT'S EYES WOULD BE SO GLAD
    ALWAYS
HE MUST FIND MY PRESENCE
A VERY GOOD DEED
WHEN I COME NEAR HIM
WATCHING
I THINK THEN
YOU COULD ASK FOR SOME TIME OR
PAINFUL SIGHT
I SEE I KEEP SHUTTING
I SHALL PUT THE WHOLE JOKE OUT THE WINDOW
AND ONE DAY I SHALL BRING FORGIVENESS

The degenerating anatomic structures
of your body

I move from blank mouth to empty face.
Things don't get better, they get worse.
And you know what that feels like.
(I made myself a lullaby once.)
Everything that came out was pre-deleted.
I presented it anyway, with a flourish.
The river is scratched out, mother,
and the people who want to live here,
they won't survive. This is where it happened,
in the hottest part of the desert,
I never went there. I pretended your body
had nothing to do with it. Stop, because,
your actual bones exist, and if I could,
I would bear them with a fiery zeal,
with the fury of all dead mothers' children
I would bear your actual bones, and I do.

I have already said that the baby appreciates,
    perhaps from the very beginning,
    the *aliveness* of the mother

We all have to die sometime, Your Majesty

Procession

Once I had a day mother

Now I have a night mother

Mourners no longer murmuring

In the late afternoon

*

They say we are doomed to repeat ourselves

So I threw away my fate

The sun went in behind a cloud and all the daffodils darkened

*

Relics of ancient rituals

A house by the sea with no view of the sea

No lamps burning at this hour

*

Every day the loss of light

The new year comes in, carrying all my language

I do not know if it is bringing or taking away

*

Last time, last time . . .

I might feel infinitely wise and as though it must show from a
    certain angle

When I saw the sea after many months it was such a meeting

Numerous dreams about rain, flooding, and bathing

*

Once I saw my mother rowing

At night across water

I called to her and she looked back

Smiling beautifully

The Forms of Resistance

Is this mountain all rock, or are there any villages on it?
These are some of the things I said to her.

We bake because it is a way of overcoming.
In the journey of zest, I see myself.

On the news every day people are standing up screaming
or lying down screaming while others remain calm.

She pointed out that I had not made eye contact
with her at all. Then I cried properly in a short burst.

This is the worst example of any circumstance ever,
noted a journalist in his notebook.

Let butter and chocolate be a wish not to die!
I implored the bain-marie. She likened me to a sieve.

I clutch all my poems to my chest and count them
again and again. I am kneeling, like a small dog.

What's going on with this modern world
and the right wife not even knowing

what the left wife is doing? Now all you have to do
is cut off the legs. After an absence, after a hard task,

after the way the hand turns, like this—
There was so much I couldn't contain.

She asked me how I was feeling in my body
at this moment; I said tense in my whole trunk area.

A strong smell of white wine. She said it came from
an impulse that she often used to have when she first

started practising. She said she believed feelings
are held in the body. She asked me what was going on

with my breath and I realised I was sort of holding it.
Like the boxes in the cupboard. 'Enough' can get bigger.

How much bigger, though? When I say
I've had enough, how will you know when to stop?

Aura

Listen to me   little water
I called you up   believing something
would arise   in me believing
I could make   you reappear
on my way   to the cemetery
every face was   luminous
as if they knew   something about
the dark   I think you
were in us all   reminding me not
to despair or if   despairing know
that we did not   lose each other
either side   of the calamity
we fused   you went inside
& I could not   see you
but afterwards   afterwards
I could see   underwater I
could see in the dark   I could see
with my eyes closed   I could see past
the shimmer that   separates the living
& the dead I knew there was nothing
no separation   it was just
aura the most   remarkable
sadness &   if only I would
keep looking   I would see you

Ghost Dance

In an age of darkness, long ago and far away, during periods of
mourning, the living would attack the dead, throwing stones at
them, hurling abuse at them, spitting and screaming with rage,
for they felt they'd been abandoned to the terrors of the night . . .

~

I woke with the whole show in my arms
Everything . . . very . . . porous, I said to myself
I am floating off

When will you come to me in my dream?
I dreamt the empty house, and I was so afraid of your ghost

Yesterday at your grave I wanted to get into bed with you,
into your daffodil bed – Mama,
because someone remembers you, you look
beautiful in spring   I addressed you
for the first time this year
you did not answer
you were shy   or angry
What do we know of the emotions of the dead? Nothing

All this time, and desire ceases to be particular
I had forgotten what it was like to want
And then I noticed the difference

I only wanted to think some thoughts with you,
but I became seduced by absence, always
asking 'What if I was a whole person?'
so they would tell me *No person is broken*,
and I'd be crying with all the pieces in my hands, but
none of these pieces is you

We enjoy, sometimes, dismantlement
I keep thinking I may find you but
I must let you go, I must let you go

Or is it you that must let *me* go

It is perfectly true that she obsessed me,
in spite of the fact that she died when I was thirteen,
until I was forty-four. A mother's death lasts a lot of years
What shall we do?

Every morning I wash my hands in the sink of your death
Melodrama doesn't suit me but I don it for character
Hahaha they say there are reasons to live
Throw me to the wolves (if there are any wolves)
She was living and now she is dead

In my mouth I can taste it   the last promise of the body
Is it only so we can keep going, these
sudden presentiments of bleakness? Yours were revolutionary
And then it all shuts down

~

Once, I was not sure I was capable of loving
Then I was too capable
Part of my story is sad
Other parts are aspirational

I cannot tell what I should choose
Whether to speak straight into the camera or keep my back to it
Whether to distort my voice when I say the difficult thing

I caught sight of her, or thought I did –
in the arms of my grandfather at the end of the war,
or holding a wine glass in a garden

Distortion is one way of making sense of things, she said,
which seemed too easy, but I wasn't even born yet,
I hadn't learned the art of asking questions

~

I wanted to tell her *You don't even know me!* to get rid of the
feeling of being known, and I wanted to keep the feeling, I
wanted to keep her, I wanted to tell her how much it hurt, and
ask her how much it hurt, I wanted to ask her how someone
known can become strange, and how a stranger could become
my familiar

~

ME ONE: Pausing on the threshold, isn't that after all where we all—
ME TWO: [*frightened*] What does it look like?
ME ONE: Well . . . a chasm. Yes, pretty much so
ME TWO: 'James James Morrison Morrison—'
ME ONE: 'Weatherby George Dupree!'
ME TWO: 'Took great care of his mother—'
ME ONE + ME TWO: 'THOUGH HE WAS ONLY THREE!'
ME ONE: [*reading*] 'Oh, it's more of a problem for them later than it is when it first happens. Tell them that right now. They think more, more of it when they become older [*becoming teary-eyed*] than they ever did when they were young [*voice shaking*]'

~

I go to the door of the house
I go to the door of the house
I, with my father, go to the door of the house

~

There was a child in my head
I asked her these questions, or she asked me them
Whenever I came to see her, she was waiting, the tyrant
She was so small, but she knew everything

~

BAMBI'S MOTHER WAS SHOT AND KILLED DURING
BAMBI'S FIRST WINTER. THESE ARE THE DANGERS OF
LIFE AS A FOREST CREATURE

~

WILDFIRE

~

What do you remember?

Nothing. They touched me in various places and asked me if it
hurt. I said no. They did not ask if it hurt when they did not touch
me. I stroked her hair but it might have been my hair I can't
remember. I read the letters of condolence. In the letters I was
'Poor Little'. In life I was a young stag. I strode through town with
my insides on the outside but they said my open wound was not
apparent. *In short, I became a cautious, housebound child, doing
what I was asked, never straying far from righteousness*

Did it hurt when they did not touch you?

~

When we lose something it seems it must be wilful
We were not paying attention
All you have to do not to lose something
is to keep it with you, so
how did this   logically   occur

~

I think of this story as the horror of forgetting
Little by little, forgetting will consume you entirely
You will become a song

~

I watched the day run down the pane
I read: 'A writer is someone for whom writing is more difficult . . .'
I wrote: 'Help me because I stutter in writing . . .'
These are the poems I have not written about my mother's death
This one's called 'We All Lived'

~

The great glass dome at the end of the station was blazing with light
It was partly that my mother's death unveiled and intensified;
made me suddenly develop perceptions, as if a burning glass
had been laid over what was shaded and dormant . . .

And when the water poured into your mouth
I begged you to forgive me,
forgive us all, forgive yourself,
but the sea was too loud

~

In your ear I whisper many answers
I do not know the questions
My self is a river, yours is a sea
When the waves hit the shore they say something unrepeatable

A river cannot survive in the sea
I was cold at first and you were warm
You took me over and I lost my temperature
You took me over and I cried the way a sea cries
I cried the way the sea cries when it has swallowed a river

~

Why is it that I can no longer bear travelling?
Why is it that I keep trying, like a lost child, to 'get home'?

~

Over a period of weeks I had a series of dreams about someone I had never met but felt sure I would meet in the future. She was a musician and the music she made, using a combination of ancient instruments and modern technology, was exquisitely painful. Every time I dreamed of her, which was almost nightly, I woke up devastated that she had yet to appear in my waking life. One day I was sitting on a bench in the local park and saw a little girl, about three or four years old. She fell over and was helped to her feet by her father. He was matter-of-fact about it and did not ask if she was okay. She was rubbing her palms together as if they were sore, but with a kind of curiosity, saying thoughtfully to herself: '*Sandy*'. I caught her eye and waved. She gazed at me for some time but did not return the wave. While she and her father were walking away she turned back once or twice and stared at me intently

~

People can be removed from the world
They don't tell you that, but it's true
I mean, they do tell you, but they don't tell you
People you love can be removed from the world
(They can remove themselves)
They will be removed from the world
Didn't anybody ever tell you that

Canopy

The weather was inside.

The branches trembled over the glass as if to apologise; then they thumped and they came in.

And the trees shook everything off until they were bare and clean. They held on to the ground with their long feet and leant into the gale and back again.

This was their way with the wind.

They flung us down and flailed above us with their visions and their pale tree light.

I think they were telling us to survive. That's what a leaf feels like anyway. We lay under their great awry display and they tattooed us with light.

They got inside us and made us speak; I said my first word in their language: 'canopy'.

I was crying and it felt like I was feeding. Be my mother, I said to the trees, in the language of trees, which can't be transcribed, and they shook their hair back, and they bent low with their many arms, and they looked into my eyes as only trees can look into the eyes of a person, they touched me with the rain on their fingers till I was all droplets, till I was a mist, and they said they would.

Day is not a tonic.

Night is not a tonic.

The cold fell off the window and on to the bed and

I was there, left behind under.

the moon.

Acknowledgements

Thank you to the editors of the following publications in which some of these poems first appeared: *BODY, Fungiculture, Granta, Kakania, London Review of Books, Morning Star, New Statesman, Poetry, Poetry International, Poetry London, Poetry Review* and *tender*.

Thank you to the following writers whose words found their way into some of these poems: Nicholas Abraham and Maria Torok, Al Alvarez, Roland Barthes, Sandra L. Bloom, John Bowlby, Marguerite Duras, Sigmund Freud, Kelly Howell, Dennis Klass, D. H. Lawrence, Christopher Lukas, Ken McMullan, Thomas Mann, A. A. Milne, Paula Neuss, Wilfred Owen, Adam Phillips, D. W. Winnicott, Virginia Woolf.

Thank you to Jeremy Noel-Tod and Denise Riley, and to the University of East Anglia for a studentship which supported me to write these poems.

Thank you to Matthew Hollis, Martha Sprackland, Emma Cheshire and Kate Burton at Faber.

Thank you and much love to my family, friends and advisers (spiritual, poetic or otherwise), especially Peter Barry, Neil Berry, Gill Shepherd, Victoria Gray and Hannah Loizos; Sarah Harrison, Rosie Dove, Anna Jones, Lois Lee, Becky Hendry, Claire Cordier, Nevena Pecotic, Adam Ferner and Natalya Anderson; Wayne Holloway-Smith, Heather Phillipson and Jack Underwood.

This book is in memory of my mother.